The Introductory
Helicopter Flying Lesson

The Introductory Helicopter Flying Lesson

Jeremy M. Pratt

Airplan Flight Equipment Limited

Published by:
Airplan Flight Equipment Limited
1a Ringway Trading Estate,
Shadowmoss Road, Manchester M22 5LH

Tel: 0161 499 0023   Fax: 0161 499 0298

e-mail: afe@airplan.u-net.com   www.airplan.u-net.com

Contents

What is an Introductory Lesson?

According to the Civil Aviation Authority (CAA), who regulate flying training in the UK, the introductory lesson is Exercise 3 of the training course for a Private Pilot's Licence (Helicopters) – abbreviated to PPL (H). In case you're wondering, Exercises 1 & 2 consist of instruction on the ground about the helicopter itself and procedures before and after flight. Exercise 3 is also known as the trial lesson or air experience flight, which is a good description of what this flight is about. It is the chance to get airborne in a small helicopter and to try your hand at flying it under the supervision of a flying instructor.

So, that is what an introductory lesson is; there are a couple of things that it is not. An introductory lesson is not the same as a pleasure flight around some local landmark, where you sit in the back and the pilot is, in effect, an aerial chauffeur. The introductory lesson is a flight where you get to do some actual piloting, it is an introduction to the art of flying a helicopter. Nor is the introductory lesson an irrevocable commitment to learn to fly. Plenty of people take an introductory lesson just for the experience, as you might try sailing a boat or driving a racing car just the once. There is nothing wrong with that at all – even though some pilots find it difficult to believe that anyone could resist the appeal of becoming a helicopter pilot! Beware though, flying helicopters can be addictive. There are plenty of pilots who got started by having an introductory lesson just for the fun of it, and found themselves hooked!

Many flying schools offer introductory lessons of differing durations, 30 or 60 minutes are typical options. The introductory lesson voucher (if there is one) may state the duration of the lesson, and the flying school staff will be pleased to confirm this for you. A flight officially starts from the moment the helicopter first leaves its parking spot under its own power, and it officially ends when the rotor blades are next stopped. This is the basis of the 'flight time' that pilots record in their logbooks and so it is normally this time that the flying school charges for.

If you are seriously thinking of learning to fly, it is worth knowing that the flying time on this flight *does* count towards the total required for completing the PPL (H) course, of which more later. If you buy a logbook at the time of the introductory lesson the instructor will help you enter the details of your flight, and you will have logged your first flight time on the way to becoming a helicopter pilot.

A pilot's logbook

The Flying Instructor,
The Helicopter,
The Flying School

Your introductory lesson will be flown with a fully licensed flying instructor. Unlike learning to drive, for example, you cannot learn to fly with anybody just because they are a qualified pilot. Even if your best friend flies helicopters all day, every day; if he or she is not a licensed flying instructor then they cannot teach you to fly – not even an introductory lesson.

To become a flying instructor, a pilot first has to amass a minimum number of flying hours and obtain certain ratings. After meeting the flying experience qualifications, an aspiring helicopter instructor has to undertake a flying instructor course (which even on a full-time basis will take at least a month) and pass a test at the end. To remain qualified, instructors undergo renewal tests every 25 months. The qualifying requirements are such that in fact, most (but not all) flying instructors are commercial pilots as well.

Aside from these qualifications flying instructors, like any other cross-section of people, come in all shapes and sizes. Your flying instructor may be a full-time professional pilot who instructs in their spare time, or a part-time pilot who instructs at weekends only, or a dedicated full-time instructor. What all flying instructors share is a real commitment to flying. It requires a certain amount of dedication (and usually their own hard-earned cash) to become an instructor – not every pilot has the ability, or the desire, to achieve an instructor rating. Instructors are almost invariably keen to pass on their knowledge and enthusiasm for flying and they are, after-all, there to help you learn.

The helicopter you will be flying in will be some type of single engine training aircraft: the Robinson R22, Enstrom F28 and Hughes/Schweizer 300 are popular training machines. Of these, the Robinson R22 is undoubtedly the type most commonly found at flying schools. Not all

Left to right:
An Enstrom F28 and a
Hughes 369

A Robinson R22

helicopter types are approved to be used for flying training, and larger types such as the ubiquitous Jet Ranger are rarely used as training machines for cost reasons. The training helicopter will have dual flying controls, as indeed virtually all helicopters have. The flying controls are explained in more detail later. To be used for flying instruction the helicopter must be maintained to a more rigorous schedule than one utilised solely for private use. It will be maintained by licensed engineers at a CAA-approved organisation, and it has to be inspected and serviced at regular intervals. On the side of the helicopter will be its registration letters, for example G-ABCD. Pilots tend to identify individual helicopters of a fleet by the last two letters of its registration, using the phonetic alphabet, so G-ABCD would be known as "Golf – Alpha Bravo Charlie Delta" – or just "Charlie Delta". This is the identification usually used as the radio callsign too.

A Squirrel helicopter with the registration letters G-OBAC "Golf – Oscar Bravo Alpha Charlie"

A training helicopter is, as you would expect, relatively docile and easy to fly. Nevertheless, it will almost certainly cruise comfortably at 100 mph or so. Because helicopters fly (mostly) in straight lines, even a relatively slow helicopter can fly some way in a short space of time, you may be surprised how fast you cover the ground even during a brief local flight. Although the helicopter you fly may be capable of climbing to above 10,000 feet, you can expect to fly not much above 2000 feet or so during the introductory lesson.

On first acquaintance a light helicopter can look, frankly, frail – especially if your previous experience of flying has been limited to airliners! In this case appearances are deceptive. A helicopter is a very strong machine, and it is built and maintained to a much higher standard than a car. It may well be certified to speeds well in excess of 100 mph, and flight loads of several times gravity (g). Even at these limits, the helicopter structure has plenty of strength in reserve, and during a normal flight it will not come anywhere close to its certified limits. It is quite possible that the helicopter you will be flying in is used regularly for flights of a hundred miles or more.

The flying school provides the facilities for proper flying instruction, and may offer a very wide range of flying courses including training for commercial licences and ratings. Those responsible for the smooth running of the school on a day-to-day basis are often referred to as the 'ground staff' or 'operations', and these unsung heroes will normally be your first point of contact at the flying school. These people have a lot to do in a busy flying school – everything from answering the phone and making the coffee, to organising the flying schedule and ensuring that the helicopters are refuelled. Many operations staff in flying schools are aspiring professional pilots themselves.

In charge of flying standards and the flying staff there will be a Chief Flying Instructor – CFI. This person will be an experienced instructor and probably an examiner too. In matters concerning flying the CFI normally has the final word! Unless your lesson has already been booked, it may be necessary to contact the flying school to fix a date and time to fly. It is worth bearing in mind that weekends are often heavily booked as this is the most popular time of the week to fly: at a particularly busy flying school, Saturdays and Sundays may be booked several weeks in advance. Although it can be worth phoning to see if you can book a lesson at short notice, there is generally a much better chance of finding a 'slot' convenient for yourself if you can fly during the week, or book well in advance at weekends.

Before You Arrive at the Flying School

With your lesson booked and confirmed with the flying school, you only have to wait for the big day to come round. On the day itself the first point to remember is that flying training, and particularly a first lesson, is very reliant on the weather conditions. It is always advisable to call the flying school before you set-out to check that the weather is suitable, as this could save you a wasted journey. Even if the sun is shining and there is not a cloud in the sky over your house, a fog patch at the airfield or thick haze may force a cancellation, so do check ahead. Safety, first and foremost, is the criteria that will decide if the weather is suitable for flying, and no self-respecting flying instructor will take you flying if she or he thinks the weather will make it too difficult for you to learn anything. If the flying school does have to cancel your lesson you can do no more than be patient, and book another appointment. Conversely, even if the weather looks dreadful where you are, it is still worth checking with the flying school. The weather may be better at the airfield, or they may take the opportunity to show you around the school and its helicopters, postponing your actual flight to another day.

A rain shower and associated rainbow seen from 2000 feet

In a modern training helicopter there is no need for any special clothing, so whatever you wear in the car on the way to the airfield should be suitable to wear in the helicopter. The only particular point is not to wear high heels, just as you would not for driving a car. The flying suits, goggles and helmets much beloved of countless old flying movies are nowhere to be seen, and you will not wear a parachute. Nor will you need to wear an oxygen mask. During this flight you are unlikely to fly much above

2000 feet, and extra oxygen does not become necessary until flying above 10-12,000 feet.

All-in-all, the general advice is 'come as you are'. The only area which may need to considered more closely concerns alcohol. The consumption of even the smallest amount of alcohol is highly inadvisable before a flying lesson. At higher altitudes the effect of any amount of alcohol is magnified greatly. All airlines will refuse boarding to drunk passengers because of the danger they pose to the aircraft's crew and passengers, and in a small helicopter the potential consequences are no less serious. Most flying schools will refuse point blank to allow someone who has been drinking into one of their helicopters. Safety is, after all, the first and foremost consideration in flying and even aside from the safety issue, you are highly unlikely to get much enjoyment from a flight under these circumstances. By the same token, flying with a hangover is not to be recommended.

If you are not feeling well for any reason don't hesitate to ring the flying school and cancel the lesson – you can always fly another day. You should also consider if you are at all susceptible to epilepsy. Under certain lighting conditions the helicopter's rotating blades can cause a 'flicker' effect in the cockpit. If you are in any doubt about this, you should take professional medical advice well in advance of a planned flight.

If you do have to cancel your lesson for whatever reason, all flying schools will appreciate the maximum notice you can give so that they have the best chance of releasing the helicopter for somebody else. To operate efficiently the flying school has to make good utilisation of its fleet, and a helicopter sitting on the ground waiting for a person who doesn't appear is a very expensive and frustrating proposition for a flying school. It's also hard on instructors, who tend to be paid by the flying hour.

On a brighter note, if you have been given an introductory lesson voucher, don't forget to take it with you as the flying school may want it. And if you have a camera you might want to take that along as well. Even the least photogenic flying instructor will normally be happy to pose with you beside the helicopter you fly in!

Before Getting to the Helicopter

Once you arrive at the flying school you can go to the reception desk and the operations staff will let you know if there are any delays or hold ups. Flying schools all try their best to keep to schedule, but are susceptible to weather problems or operational delays that can throw an otherwise well-running flying schedule into confusion.

At this stage you will probably be asked to fill-out a simple membership form that makes you a temporary member of the flying school. This is a fairly standard procedure and is something that the school's insurance company probably insist on. It is a sad fact of life that we live in increasing litigious times, and so even at this early stage of your flying career such mundane matters intrude.

All being well, you will now meet your instructor. He or she might well ask if you live locally, and it may be possible to route the flight accordingly. However, be aware that the helicopter is unlikely to fly very far from the airfield in a short flight, it is not always possible to see your home from the air. Your instructor will also give you an overview of the weather situation and the expected format for the flight. You will probably receive some form of pre-flight briefing, to give you an idea of how to fly the helicopter and what will be covered in this lesson. Many instructors will be interested to know if this is just a one-off experience, or if you are seriously thinking of taking-up helicopter flying. They can then format the flight so that you can get the best out of it. At this stage, and throughout the flight, you should feel free to ask any questions that spring to mind, or query anything that you do not fully understand. Remember – your instructor is there to help you, and there's no such thing as a stupid question, only a stupid answer! Like many other professions, flying has a wide range of vocabulary and 'buzz-words' all of its own. Many people in the flying business use these words and expressions without conscious effort, but don't hesitate to ask someone to spell-out anything incomprehensible. To help, there is a glossary and list of abbreviations at the back of this book.

Before leaving the flying school building the instructor will complete the necessary paperwork formalities and may need to telephone the Air Traffic Control (ATC) unit on the airfield to give them details of the flight. Then it's time to walk-out to the helicopter, a time when some people start to wonder just what they've let themselves in for!

Out at the helicopter the instructor will probably first get you seated in the helicopter. Getting in (and out) of the cockpit is usually very simple, and your instructor will show you any hand holds to use, and help you to avoid banging the controls or knocking any switches.

Sometimes you may be taken out to a helicopter with the rotor blades already turning, a so-called 'running change'. In this instance you will accompanied by a member of the flying school staff who will show you how to approach the helicopter. Follow this advice closely: in general the two most important points are to duck low when under the rotor

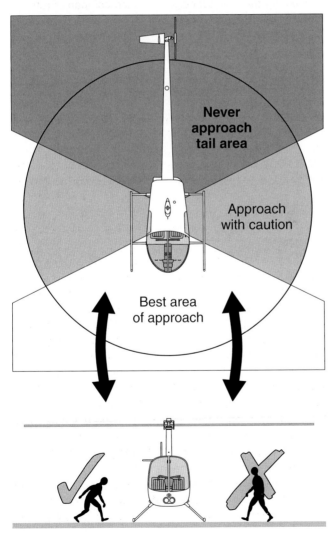

Never approach tail area

Approach with caution

Best area of approach

Never approach a helicopter's tail area, and always duck low when walking under moving rotor blades

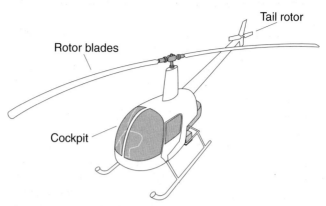

Tail rotor

Rotor blades

Cockpit

blades, and to avoid completely the tail area of the helicopter. Remember too that the airflow under the rotating blades will blow around any loose clothing and a hat or cap if you are wearing one.

Once in the cockpit, your instructor will help you get settled into your seat. You will probably be sitting on the right-hand side of the helicopter, as for most helicopter types the right-side seat is where the captain (or Pilot In Command, it's the same thing) sits. As a trainee pilot you occupy this seat because you are training to fly as a Pilot In Command, and so most of the instruments and switches will be in front of you or on a central panel.

The three flying controls – the cyclic stick, collective lever and pedals

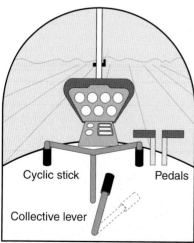

Cyclic stick

Pedals

Collective lever

In front of you will be two of the flying controls – a 'stick' coming up from the floor and pedals for your feet. The 'stick' is known as the 'cyclic' and can take two forms. There may be two cyclic sticks, one in front of each seat, which are interconnected so that moving one stick makes the other move in the same way. Alternatively there may be one cyclic stick that is positioned between the seats, with a dual 'handle-bar' type grip on top, meaning that either pilot can move the cyclic stick. The cyclic controls the attitude of the helicopter, i.e. its angle in relation to the horizon. Forward and back pressure on the cyclic makes the helicopter pitch down (forward pressure) or pitch up (back pressure) as seen from the cockpit. Moving the stick from side to side makes the helicopter bank to the left when the cyclic is moved to the left, and right when the cyclic is moved to the right.

The pedals are on the floor, with a left and a right pedal, one for each foot. The pedals control the helicopter in yaw – making the helicopter rotate from side to side as seen from the cockpit. Pressing the left pedal rotates the helicopter to the left, and vice versa.

The third flying control, which you may not notice at first glance, is a lever – rather like a car handbrake – at the left side of the seat. This control is known as the 'collective' lever, and it has a 'twist grip' at the end. Pulling the collective up makes the helicopter rise, lowering it makes the helicopter descend. The twist grip is the engine throttle, it is twisted anti-clockwise to increase engine power and twisted clockwise to decrease engine power.

This description of the flying controls is rather basic, but will do for now, whilst we are still on the ground.

Once in your seat the instructor will show you how to adjust the seat, if the seat is fitted for such adjustment. The most important factor is that you should be able to reach the flying controls easily, without having to stretch out, and you should also be able to see over the instrument panel. Once airborne you will control the helicopter by reference to the view ahead, so it is worth spending a few moments now to make sure that you have an unobstructed view and a good reach on the flying controls. The flying school may well be able to provide extra seat cushions to help in this respect.

At this stage, the instructor may leave the cockpit to walk around the helicopter, carrying out the pre-flight checks (alternatively these may have been done before taking you out to the aircraft, and also will not be necessary if the helicopter is already running when you get to it). The pre-flight checks are an established ritual in flying, and apply just as much to an airliner about to make a transcontinental flight, as to a single engine helicopter about to fly once around the airfield. The instructor will make a circuit around the helicopter, prodding, shaking, peering and examining various bits and pieces to satisfy him/herself that it is fit to fly.

A pilot 'pre-flighting' a Robinson R22

Even if the helicopter has only just shut down from a previous flight, the pilot about to take it will always perform this check. Don't be alarmed if you see the instructor muttering or mumbling to him/herself during the pre-flight check. Many pilots do this (most without realising it), they're narrating the things they are checking, as if reciting a poem learnt off by heart!

You may have a spare minute to look at the instrument panel in front of you. Do not be put off even if it seems to be filled with incomprehensible dials, indicators and instruments. You will only need to refer to a few of these during the flight, and mostly you will control the helicopter by reference to the view outside. The five principle flight instruments in a helicopter are:

The Heading Indicator, which indicates the aircraft's heading in degrees of the compass (also sometimes known as the Direction Indicator – DI).

The Altimeter, which shows height of the helicopter above a fixed datum, the usual reference is sea level.

The Airspeed Indicator, which measures the airflow and displays this in terms of speed through the air.

The Vertical Speed Indicator which shows the rate at which the helicopter is climbing or descending in hundreds of feet per minute.

The rotor RPM gauge, which displays the RPM (Revolutions Per Minute) of the rotor blades, a major factor in helicopter performance and control.

You may also notice the compass, often mounted above the instrument panel.

Of these instruments, the Airspeed Indicator, the Heading Indicator and the Altimeter are probably of most interest during the introductory lesson, and so are worth looking at a little more closely.

An AirSpeed Indicator – ASI

The Airspeed Indicator measures the pressure of the airflow from a sensing point known as the pitot. The pressure sensed is converted by the instrument into a measurement of speed, and displayed by a needle which moves around the instrument dial. The dial will be commonly calibrated in miles·per hour (mph), or knots. A knot is a nautical mile, which is slightly longer than the statute mile measured on a car speedometer, for example 90 knots is equivalent to about 100 mph. Knots are used for navigational reasons, and wind speed is also mostly given in knots. The airspeed is an important determinant of performance, and you will find that a pilot pays particular attention to the Airspeed Indicator throughout the flight.

The Heading Indicator contains a gyroscope, and is set by reference to the compass. When correctly set, the Heading Indicator will show the direction in which the helicopter is pointing. The dial is divided into degrees around the points of the compass, where north is 360°, east is 90°,

A Heading Indicator

south is 180° and west is 270°. The Heading Indicator is normally marked around the rim with lines every 10°, and a shorter line for intermediate 5°.

The altimeter senses the air pressure outside the helicopter and converts this into an indication of altitude, on the basis that pressure decreases with height. The dial

An Altimeter

of the altimeter will have two pointers: a long pointer which indicates hundreds of feet, and a shorter one that indicates thousands of feet. The altimeter will also have a small 'window' in which a set of numbers is visible, this is called the 'sub-scale'. The setting in the sub-scale window is set by use of a small knob next to the face of the altimeter. Because pressure changes constantly as weather systems move across the globe, the altimeter has to be reset regularly for it to give an accurate

reading. Before take-off, the instructor will obtain a pressure setting called 'QNH', and set this number on the altimeter sub-scale. When QNH is set, the altimeter will indicate the helicopter's altitude above sea level, for example on the ground at the airfield it should display the airfield's elevation above sea level. When returning to the airfield to land, the altimeter setting will probably be changed to QFE. When QFE is set, the altimeter will indicate the helicopter's height above the airfield.

With the instructor seated beside you, you will be shown how to fasten and adjust the seat belt/harness. There is no need for this to be breathtakingly tight; a snug, comfortable fit is just right. The instructor will also show you how to release the seat belt/harness, how to open the door or other exit, and point-out any particular safety features. This is the equivalent of the safety briefing you will have seen if you have flown as a passenger in an airliner, and your instructor will appreciate it if you pay attention!

The instructor will now run through the pre-starting checks, probably with the aid of a checklist. The pre-starting checks will include moving the flight controls and setting certain switches and selectors. Items such as the instruments and ancillary controls will also be checked now, in preparation for starting the engine.

Once the engine is running, the rotor blades will begin to turn. It will take a short time for them to reach operating RPM; the noise level will increase and there may be some vibration as the rotors pass through certain RPM values. During this time you will put on a headset as used in all modern training helicopters. The headset is simply a set of headphones that go over the ears, with a microphone mounted on a boom that is positioned in front of the mouth. The instructor will show you how to adjust the headband so that the ear cups sit snugly on your head. There is no need to tighten the headband so that your head is gripped like a vice, but you do want it secure enough not to slip off. Move the headband so that it sits right on the crown of your head for best comfort. The microphone is positioned by moving the boom so that the microphone is just in front of your lips, say about 1.5

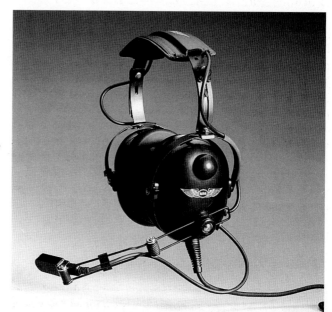

A typical headset, note the volume control on the side of the ear-cup

inches away. There may well be a volume control on the ear cup, so that you can adjust the volume to suit.

Once you are wearing the headset, with the radio on, you should be able to hear the conversation between other aircraft and ATC on the radio, and also the voice of your instructor (and your own voice) via the intercom. There is no need to press any button to speak on the intercom, the microphone will either be permanently 'live', or voice activated. With the headset on and properly adjusted you should be able to carry on a conversation with the instructor at normal speaking levels. To transmit a message over the radio, the instructor will press a transmit button (sometimes labelled PTT – Press To Talk), which is often mounted on the cyclic grip. Unlike a telephone, radio communication is a 'one-way' process, only one person can talk at a time. You may see the instructor listening out and waiting for a gap in radio transmissions before pressing the PTT button to transmit a message. Although the intercom does make conversation within the helicopter very easy, the background chatter of the radio can be a bit of distraction. Most experienced pilots have the knack of being constantly aware of what is being said on the radio, turning their full attention to it when a message relevant to their helicopter is broadcast. Occasionally the instructor may have to interrupt a conversation with you to catch something on the radio or to acknowledge a message. Don't worry if the radio messages sound like a stream of verbal nonsense. Most people find the radio like that at first, but it soon becomes quite comprehensible when you know some of the conventions and vocabulary.

The instructor will look after setting the radio frequencies: at a small airfield there may be just one radio frequency in use, whilst a larger airfield may have several frequencies, each providing a different service.

Whilst the rotor blades are reaching their operating RPM the instructor will be completing various checks within the cockpit. These checks may include verifying some of the helicopter's warning systems, and so occasionally a warning light or alarm sound may come on at this time. Once the checks are complete, and probably with a brief enquiry to yourself to see if you are ready to go, the time has come for flight!

To lift-off, the instructor will raise the collective lever by the seat. You may notice a change in engine note, and the helicopter will go light on the skids. It will then lift into a low hover, a few feet above the ground. It will stay in the hover whilst the instructor makes a few more checks before moving off. What? More checks! You will realise that a light helicopter is operated to the same standards of professionalism as a large airliner. The basic philosophy is to check rather than assume, check again just to be sure, and to take nothing for granted in the meantime!

Once the instructor is satisfied, and ready to move off, what happens next will depend on airfield procedures. At some airfields, the helicopter will 'hover taxy', hovering along slowly a few feet above the ground, to a specified point from where it can climb-out away from the airfield. Alternatively, the helicopter may be able to climb-out directly from over its parking spot.

In either case, when ready to climb-out the instructor will probably line-up the helicopter to face into wind. Just about everything that flies tries to take-off and land as closely as possible into the wind, this applies just as much to a Boeing 747 as to a small training helicopter. Taking-off into wind increases controllability and gives the helicopter a steeper climb gradient after take-off. You may see the instructor look at the windsock to check the wind, and the wind speed and direction may also be passed over the radio, for example "Surface wind 240 degrees, 10 knots". Contrary to what you may expect, it is highly unlikely that the helicopter will climb-out vertically. Although it is capable of doing this, it is not the most efficient way to climb. Instead, after a final inquiry to yourself to make sure that you are ready to fly, the instructor will radio ATC for permission to climb-out (this is not always necessary at a small airfield). Then, after a final look around; the instructor will lower the nose of the helicopter and it will begin to move forward with increasing speed. This change from the stationery hover to forward flight is called the 'transition'. At a certain airspeed, the helicopter will start climbing. As you cross the airfield boundary, and the ground falls away, your first helicopter flying lesson has begun.

How Helicopters Fly

Most people who have more than a passing interest in helicopters are apt to wonder from time to time what forces are at work to make the whole business of helicopter flight possible. Even a qualified helicopter pilot, watching several tonnes of helicopter hovering around with little apparent effort, is sometimes prone to think the same way!

Before going any further it ought to be stated here that a knowledge of the basic principles of flight, as instructors like to call the process that keeps a helicopter airborne, is not essential at this stage. After all, birds fly perfectly well without ever having been instructed in the mysteries of lift, drag etc. Likewise, the early pioneer pilots managed quite well before many of the principles of flight were fully understood. If you are quite happy to accept that helicopters fly because that's what they are designed to do (and there's plenty of evidence to show that this is true) then feel free to skip this section. However, if you have an interest in the processes involved, a little basic knowledge could help you get much more from your introductory flight.

It is useful to begin by looking at how a 'fixed-wing' aircraft flies. The principle force at work which allows an aircraft to fly, rather than just ploughing off the end of the runway as a surface vehicle would, is *lift*.

Lift is generated by the aircraft's wings, and in normal level flight the wings are generating an amount of lift equal to the weight of the aircraft. Thus, if a typical light aircraft weighs 700kg (1540lbs or thereabouts), its wings must generate 700kg of lift to keep the aircraft flying at a constant level.

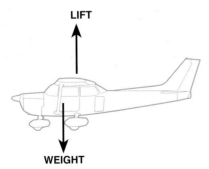

Lift opposes weight

If you look at a cross-section through a wing, you will notice a fairly distinctive 'aerofoil' shape. As the airflow reaches the wing, a combination of this shape, the airflow speed and the angle at which the airflow meets the wing, causes a difference in the speed of the airflow above and below the wing. The airflow over the wing's top surface is faster than the airflow beneath it. It is a basic property of moving air that a faster airflow speed is associated with reduced pressure (and vice versa). So, to summarise, the airflow speed and the angle at which it meets the wing creates a pressure differential – the pressure above the wing is less than the pressure below it. In essence, the wing is 'sucked' up by the reduced pressure above it, and that force is lift.

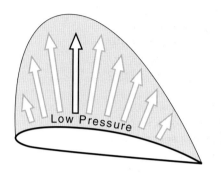

Generation of lift by the airflow around the aerofoil section

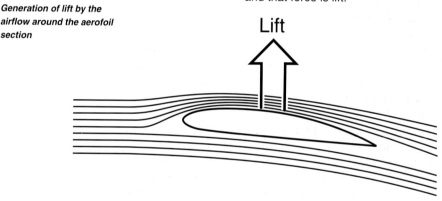

There are plenty of examples of lift outside the aviation world, for example the 'wings' on racing cars that provide lift downwards – downforce – to keep the cars pressed down onto the road at high speeds. The lift (downforce) generated by even these small surfaces can be several times greater than the weight of the car itself. Thus, in theory, such a car could drive along the roof of a tunnel, the downforce keeping it pressed onto the surface. The only problem is, if the car slows down it will generate less lift, and it may fall off – maybe this is why nobody had tried this out for real! Hydrofoils on high-speed boats are also wings, operating in water instead of air to lift the boat hull clear of the water at high speed.

If you are intrigued enough to try a small experiment, take a small, flat object (such as this book), then hold it into an airflow such as a strong wind or the airflow past a moving car (preferably whilst somebody else does the driving!). Holding it parallel to the airflow you will notice little force. Now angle it up slightly, you will start to feel the lift force: don't angle it too far, you may lose your grip on it. Of course, this book won't make a very efficient wing, and the airflow will be slower than that past an aircraft, but the basic principle is the same.

A helicopter does not have fixed wings to produce lift. In a helicopter the lifting action necessary to overcome weight is provided by the rotor blades (which, in cross section, have a similar shape as a wing). Instead of pushing the craft forward to provide an airflow over the wings, the rotor blades are rotated. The end result is the same, the movement of air past the blades provides lift. Although purists prefer to call this 'lift' by the term 'Total Rotor Thrust' in the case of helicopters, for our purposes 'lift' describes the force perfectly well. It is the control of the lift force generated by the rotor blades that gives the helicopter its ability to hover, move forwards, backwards or sideways, and do all sorts of useful things.

Think of the rotating rotor blades as a disc. In a stationary hover, the disc is providing enough lift to balance the helicopter's weight. If the pilot pulls up on the collective lever, the collective angle of the blades to the airflow increases. This increases the lift being produced by the disc, and the helicopter will rise. Lowering the collective lever reduces the collective angle of the blades, and so the lift being produced by the disc is less and the helicopter will descend.

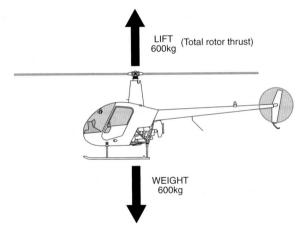

LIFT (Total rotor thrust)
600kg

WEIGHT
600kg

Moving the cyclic stick alters the angle of each blade depending on its position in its cycle, thus altering the direction of the lift force. If the pilot applies forward pressure on the cyclic stick, the nose of the helicopter lowers. Now the lift force is angled forward, and the helicopter will start to move ahead with increasing speed. Back pressure on the cyclic stick slows the helicopter and, if held after the

Forward pressure on the cyclic stick makes the helicopter pitch down

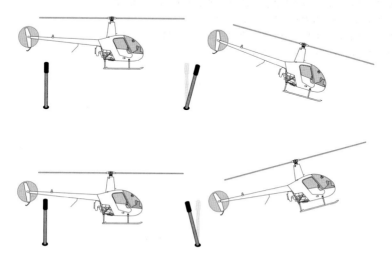

Back pressure on the cyclic stick makes the helicopter pitch up

Moving the cyclic to the left, banks the helicopter to the left, and vice versa

helicopter has come to a halt, makes it move backwards. Moving the cyclic stick to one side moves the lift force in the same direction that the cyclic is deflected to. Left cyclic makes the helicopter bank to the left and vice versa.

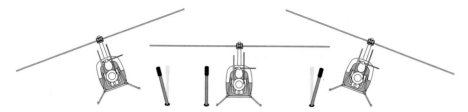

If you have a mechanical turn of mind, you may realise that having these large rotor blades spinning around will create various counter-acting forces. To stop the helicopter body from simply whirling around in the opposite direction to the blade rotation, the helicopter will have a 'tail rotor'. This is, in essence, a miniature rotor blade, mounted vertically at the back on the helicopter and powered by the engine. The tail rotor provides a force to stop the helicopter spinning around against the main rotor blade rotation. The pedals (known more properly as the 'yaw' pedals or 'anti-torque' pedals) give the pilot additional control of the tail rotor, allowing him or her to 'yaw' the helicopter around its vertical axis.

If all of this seems rather complicated, it must be said that it is a lot easier to appreciate in an airborne machine than explain on paper. Now is a good time to return to the real-life business of flying helicopters.

In the Air

There is a story about a research team who wanted to record the sensation of somebody making their first parachute jump. They found a volunteer, and spent months training him to be able to narrate the forces and sensations he was expected to experience. He was equipped with sophisticated monitoring equipment, including a miniature tape recorder he could talk into. After the necessary training the big day came, our hero climbed into the aircraft and it roared off. At the pre-arranged height he stepped out onto the strut, and then jumped.

Safely back on the ground the researchers gathered round and re-wound the recording tape in anticipation. It contained just one word: "Yiipppeeeeee!"

The point of this story is to illustrate that like any new experience, the sensation of getting airborne is a subjective one, sensed differently by different people. The feeling may be one of revelation, a dream fulfilled, possibly a little nervousness, or just mild curiosity.

A small helicopter will tend to undulate more than an airliner in any wind currents and turbulence, just as a small boat will be more affected by a sea swell than a large ship. Any movement is unlikely to be excessive, it's just a question of being a new and unknown sensation. The air tends to become smoother as you climb, and any initial nervousness will tend to disappear quickly in any case as your senses adjust to the slight movements.

If you have been used to flying just as a passenger in airliners, you may be surprised at how much visibility there is from a helicopter, sitting as you are inside a large perspex bubble. As you climb higher prominent landmarks such as mountains, woodland or nearby towns will become visible. You may be able to recognise these, if not the instructor will be pleased to point-out and name the major landmarks around. Remember, don't be afraid to ask questions: secretly most instructors are quite pleased to be able to show off their knowledge! At this early stage of the flight the instructor will be routing away from the airfield and climbing to a reasonable altitude. Take the opportunity to look around, orientate yourself and enjoy the view. You may have unintentionally tensed-up, so make a conscious effort now to relax, you will enjoy the flight much more when you do.

A motorway...

...and a small town, as seen from 1500ft

With the helicopter levelled-out and settled in the cruise, the time has come for you to try some flying for yourself.

Firstly, the instructor will demonstrate to you the effect of the flying controls. Looking ahead, you should be able to see the horizon, and the angle of the helicopter in relation to it – this is know as the *attitude*. A normal 'straight and level' attitude may look something like this:

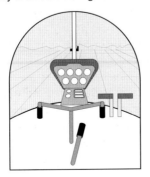

The 'normal' straight and level attitude, based on the cockpit of a Robinson R22

The instructor will now apply some back pressure to the cyclic stick. Note the phraseology here: there is no question of pulling the cyclic hard back, huge control movements are *not* the order of the day in helicopters. The total movement of the cyclic is unlikely to be anything more than an inch or so, and if you regard the input required as a pressure rather than a movement you will be thinking along the right lines. Returning to the demonstration, as the instructor applies back pressure on the cyclic, look ahead: you will see that the helicopter is pitching up gently. Compare the horizon with the reference point the instructor shows you (possibly the magnetic compass on the windscreen) to get a better idea of the attitude.

The whole demonstration is much quicker than a written description, and after applying some back pressure the new, higher attitude may look something like this:

Back pressure on the cyclic makes the helicopter pitch-up to a higher attitude

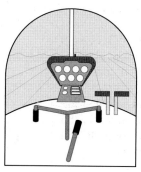

Now you can look at pitching down. All that is needed is a gentle forward pressure on the cyclic. Looking ahead you will see the helicopter pitch down gently and the new, lower attitude may look something like this:

Forward pressure on the cyclic makes the helicopter pitch-down to a lower attitude

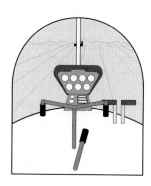

The instructor may have asked you to place your right hand *lightly* on the cyclic during the demonstration so that you can get some idea of the relationship between control movement/pressure and change in attitude. Following the demonstration in this way is known as 'following through'. Remember to think of applying a pressure to the cyclic, rather than making a large movement. The analogy is to think of the way you would handle the steering wheel of a car travelling at 100 mph or more, and treat the cyclic in the same way: it is difficult to over-emphasis this point. Now you will be invited to try out the forward and back pressure on the cyclic for yourself. The instructor will talk you through, prompting the actions needed. You have now seen that the forward and backward movement of the cyclic controls the pitch attitude of the helicopter.

Now the instructor will demonstrate the side-to-side movement of the cyclic. Looking ahead, when the cyclic is moved to the right, you will see that the helicopter banks to the right – this movement is known as roll. Again the amount of control movement needed is small, but a little more than the pressure used when controlling in pitch. With the helicopter banked to the right you may see that the helicopter turns to the right. The picture outside will look something like this:

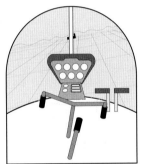

Right movement of the cyclic makes the helicopter bank and turn to the right

The instructor will return the helicopter to a level attitude, then bank the helicopter to the left by moving the cyclic to the left. Now you will see the helicopter turning to the left and the picture outside will look a bit like this:

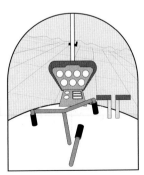

Left movement of the cyclic makes the helicopter bank and turn to the left

Again, the instructor may invite you to try this for yourself to get a feel for how the helicopter reacts to movement of the cyclic. You have now seen that moving the cyclic from side to side controls roll.

Now the instructor will demonstrate the use of the collective lever. In very crude terms you can think of the collective as an 'up and down' control. Pulling the collective lever gently up causes the helicopter to climb, lowering it allows the helicopter to descend. This far above the surface it is difficult to notice deviations in height straight away, so your instructor may point-out the indications on the altimeter and Vertical Speed Indicator (VSI) to show that the helicopter is climbing or descending. Again, when you try this for yourself the emphasis is on small and smooth control movements.

The instructor may also demonstrate the use of the yaw pedals. Pressing the right pedal causes the nose to yaw to the right, and vice versa. However, many instructors choose not to demonstrate the use of the pedals at this stage of the introductory lesson as they are not used too much for straight and level flight (which is what you are about to practice), and instead they leave the use of the pedals until later.

Now that you have seen how the cyclic is used to control the attitude of the helicopter in pitch and roll, and the use of the collective to maintain height, it is time to put this knowledge to practical use by flying the helicopter straight and level.

To demonstrate this the instructor will settle the helicopter in the 'normal' cruise, heading towards some sort of distinguishable landmark.

A constant level is maintained by keeping the helicopter at the 'normal' pitch attitude. If the attitude is too high, use forward pressure on the cyclic to return to the desired attitude. If the attitude is too low, use back pressure on the cyclic to return to the desired attitude. It is unlikely that you will need to make any adjustment to the collective lever at this stage. Once the collective is set for level flight, maintaining the correct attitude should keep the helicopter at a constant height.

The helicopter is kept flying straight by keeping it level. For example if the helicopter banks to the left, move the cyclic to the right until the helicopter is level again. If the helicopter banks to the right, move the cyclic to the left until the helicopter is level again. To assess if you are maintaining a constant direction, choose a distinctive landmark ahead. As long as it stays in the same spot relative to yourself, you are maintaining a constant direction. If the landmark moves to one side, you will need to bank the helicopter back towards it, levelling the helicopter when the landmark is ahead again.

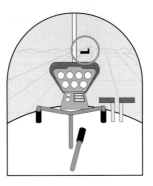

Choose a distinctive landmark ahead to confirm that you are maintaining a constant direction

All of this is far more simple to do than to read about. The control movements needed to maintain straight and level flight are as instinctive as driving a car in a straight line, with the added feature of working in three dimensions instead of two. Now you have seen what is required, you will get a chance to put it into practice.

To many people, even with the knowledge that the person sitting next to them has a full set of dual controls, the thought of the instructor relinquishing control to them is a daunting one. There is no reason to feel this way. Unlike learning to drive, where a movement of just a few feet from a given path can have unfortunate consequences, in the sky you have a lot of space to move around in. This means that the instructor can allow you to get a feel for controlling the helicopter, without having to intervene the moment the helicopter moves away from the desired flight path. In fact, the instructor will usually only intervene to change direction or height, or if you start to look worried!

It is worth remembering that in the cruise, the helicopter does not require intensive control movements, it should be able to cruise straight and level with only minimal movements of the cyclic. With this in mind, you can apply yourself to flying the helicopter.

Within a few minutes you may well find that flying the helicopter, maintaining straight and level flight, is not a complicated task, and soon becomes almost instinctive. This said, there are two common errors often made when first learning to fly; they are:

- over-controlling, and
- gripping the controls too hard.

Over-controlling happens when the pilot makes control movements much larger close that required, for example pulling back too fast and too far on the cyclic when trying to correct a too-low attitude. The result is that the helicopter pitches up too far, and suddenly you are faced with a too-high attitude. If you reverse the error (pushing forward too fast and too far) the helicopter pitches down quickly, and you have all the beginnings of a roller-coaster ride! If this happens to you simply take a deep breath, relax, and then try again, with a conscious effort to make the control movements smaller, slower and smoother. One way to avoid over-controlling on the cyclic is to rest your right arm on your leg whilst you are holding the cyclic. This should help you to avoid making excessive control inputs.

Gripping the controls too hard may also be a cause of over-controlling and may make it difficult for you to sense the pressures and movements needed on the cyclic. Look down at your hand; if it is gripping the cyclic as if your life depends on it (probably with the knuckles starting to show white), then you are holding the cyclic far too tightly. Again the solution is simple: take a deep breath, relax your grip, and try again. To avoid over-controlling try placing just your thumb and two fingers on the cyclic. This way it is more difficult to grip the cyclic too tightly, and you will be able to feel the movements of the control much better.

Because on this flight you will be staying fairly close to the airfield, you will not fly for too long in a straight line. The instructor may encourage you to make some of the turns yourself. To turn, simply move the cyclic in the desired direction. The helicopter will bank in that direction and will start to turn in the direction that you are banked to. As the helicopter is turning, apply a little back pressure on the cyclic. When you wish to stop the turn, simply level the helicopter with the cyclic, remembering to anticipate by starting to 'roll out' of the turn just before the new landmark is directly ahead.

Later in the lesson, the instructor may also give you the chance to control height with the collective lever, for example if the collective is lowered, the helicopter will start a gentle descent.

Once you feel that it is becoming easier to fly the helicopter, you may want to look at some of the instruments. The Airspeed Indicator will show the helicopter's speed through the air, a figure of 70 knots/80 mph is typical at this stage of the flight. Of course, once more than a few hundred feet above the surface there is little sensation of speed because there is nothing nearby to act as a reference. Nevertheless, if you are flying over an area you know well, you will realise how quickly the helicopter moves between points that are many road miles apart. The Heading Indicator shows the direction in which the helicopter is headed, in degrees magnetic. When flying straight, the heading should remain constant. The altimeter will indicate the aircraft's altitude. When flying at a constant level the altitude should remain constant.

Although you may want to look at the instruments for interest, do not try to fly the helicopter by sole reference to them, it is far more difficult than it looks. Even if you do manage to get one instrument, say the Heading Indicator, to read exactly as you want it; you can guarantee that some other factor, for example the altitude, will now be going wrong. Flying the helicopter by reference to the view outside is by far the best way to learn how to fly at this stage. Deviations of up to 20°-30° in heading and 200-300 feet in altitude are not usually a problem in an introductory lesson and besides, looking outside gives you a chance to enjoy the view too!

While cruising along, you may wonder what would happen if the engine were to fail. Contrary to what you might think, the rotor blades would not just stop. The rotor blades can in fact rotate free of the engine, rather like a car 'free-wheeling' with the gear in neutral and the engine turned off. In the unlikely event of an engine failure, the forward speed of the helicopter keeps the blades rotating, and a controlled descent (known as an 'autorotation') is made to an engine-off landing. This is just the sort of procedure you will practice regularly if you train for a helicopter pilot's licence.

Whilst concentrating on flying the aircraft, you will probably notice little else and the time will pass very quickly. If you do feel at all unwell, tell your instructor so that (s)he can help. As a general rule the act of flying the helicopter should still any queasy feeling, and looking ahead rather than moving your head around a lot may also help. The instructor will be able to open fresh air vents if you want. Above all, don't worry. The sensation of flying in a small helicopter can take a little getting used to, but any queasiness will soon pass.

By now your instructor will be thinking of returning to the airfield, and descending towards it. At the risk of stating the obvious, the approach to the airfield is usually just the reverse of the initial climb away from it, a question of descending and reducing airspeed towards a stationary hover a few feet above the ground. Although a helicopter

Approaching an airfield

can come to the hover at considerable altitude, and then lower down vertically to the surface, this type of approach is rarely used.

The exact lesson format will vary between flying schools, but quite often your instructor will approach an area of the airfield reserved for hovering practice, known as the 'hover square'. Within the hover square your instructor can demonstrate some of the true art of helicopter flying, such as hovering and turning over a spot, and flying backwards and sideways. Your could be forgiven for thinking that your instructor is showing off his/her flying prowess, and maybe they are. Nevertheless, instructors welcome the chance to show-off their skills, and you can indulge them by being suitably impressed at the right moments!

Conditions permitting, you may now get the chance to try controlling the helicopter in the hover. This, it must be said, is significantly more intense than controlling the helicopter in forward flight. When the helicopter is 'cruising' in straight and level flight, the airflow past the helicopter gives it a certain amount of stability. In the hover, there is no such stabilising airflow, and it is fair to say that in the hover the helicopter is, to all intents and purposes, unstable. A movement in one direction or axis will tend to continue or increase until the pilot halts it. Moreover, for various reasons, the movement of one control, will effect the actions needed on the others. This is where the skill of co-ordination really comes into its own. Whilst hovering is undoubtedly the most difficult and skillful aspect of flying a helicopter, it is also the most rewarding.

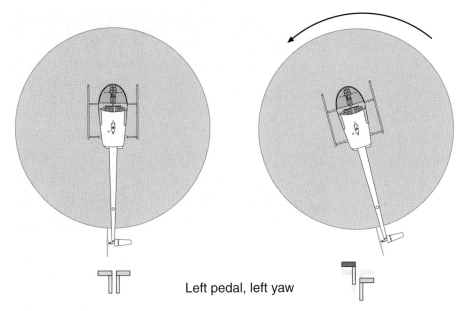

Left pedal, left yaw

To start, you will probably take control of the pedals whilst your instructor handles the other controls. The aim is the keep the helicopter pointed in the same direction, with reference to a tree or similar object ahead. Pushing the pedal to the left rotates the helicopter to the left, and vice versa. Keeping the chosen object straight ahead is likely to require constant small, movements on the pedals. This

Left pedal causes yaw to the left, right pedal causes yaw to right

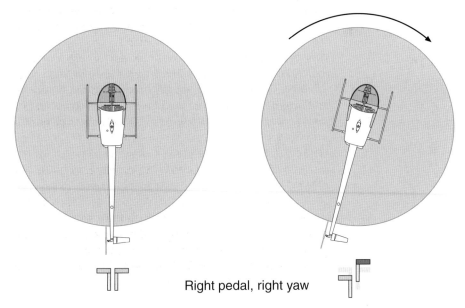

Right pedal, right yaw

Raising the collective lever makes the helicopter climb, lowering it makes the helicopter descend

is a point worth remembering. Once you have tried controlling the pedals, the instructor will probably take them over again, and allow you to try controlling the

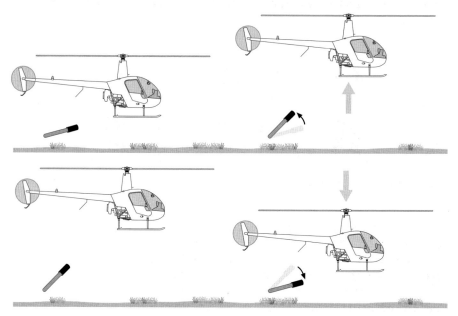

collective lever. The aim is to maintain a constant height above the ground. If the helicopter starts to descend, raising the collective lever a little will arrest the descent. If the helicopter is climbing, lowering the collective lever slightly should stop the climb. Finding the appropriate control movements is very much a case of practice and experience, don't be surprised if your instructor helps you at times. Out of interest, you might like to know that there is a linkage between the collective lever and the throttle, this means that when the collective lever is raised, power automatically increases. When the collective lever is lowered, power automatically reduces. Twisting the grip on the end of the throttle also alters engine power, but this is used more by pilots to 'fine tune' the power setting. After you have tried-out the collective, your instructor may take the all controls again and then allow you to try the cyclic control. Now is a good time to re-emphasis that in the hover, constant small, control movements are the best way to control the helicopter. The art of hovering a helicopter has been compared to that of balancing a ball bearing on the tip of a pencil. In reality it's not *that* difficult, but only training and practice makes perfect. In the hover, the aim is to stay stationary over one spot. Moving the cyclic to the side will bank the helicopter, but before that bank becomes evident, you will see that the helicopter

Moving the cyclic to the right, moves the helicopter to the right, and vice versa

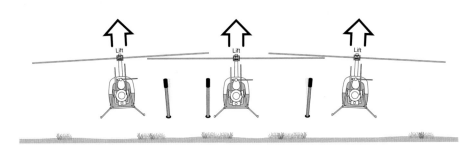

starts to move sideways in the direction to which the cyclic has been moved. Likewise, moving the cyclic forward and back will pitch the helicopter, but before that is evident the helicopter will start to move forward (forward pressure on the cyclic) or move back (back pressure on the cyclic). Bear in mind that in the hover, it is not possible to just hold the cyclic still and expect the helicopter to suddenly freeze its position in the air. A constant series of small, quick movements of the cyclic *will* be needed to keep the helicopter where you want it.

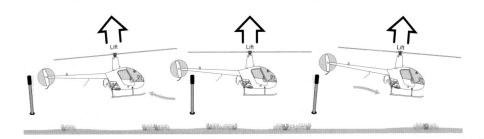

It is possible that if you and your instructor are feeling confident enough, you may have the chance to try operating all the controls at once in order to maintain the hover over a given spot, holding a constant direction and a constant height. There is little practical advice to give about this, as it is largely a matter of putting into practice the individual skills you have just been trying out. Do not be surprised if your instructor intervenes to keep things under control and keep the helicopter somewhere within the hovering square. To be fair, with just a few minutes of experience in flying a helicopter nobody could expect you to hover one perfectly, although it is great fun to try!

You are probably now approaching the end of the lesson. Your instructor will 'hover taxy' back to the parking spot, and then lower the helicopter onto the ground. After a few final checks, he or she will then close down the engine. The rotor blades will start to slow down, and your instructor may use a 'rotor brake' to bring the blades to a stop. You may find the silence quite startling after getting used to the noise of the engine and the rotor blades. All there is now is the sound of the instrument gyros running down and the occasional pinking noise as the engine cools; your first helicopter flying lesson is over.

What Now?

Back in the flying school the instructor will need to complete some paperwork formalities after flight, and there may be an introductory lesson certificate waiting for you. The flying school staff will probably ask you if you enjoyed the flight, and if you are interested in taking more lessons. This may be a difficult question to answer immediately, and you may want to know a bit more about the course and the licence it leads to.

The Private Pilot's Licence (Helicopters)

The introductory lesson is the first flying lesson of the course for the Private Pilot's Licence (Helicopters). Before looking at the training course, it makes sense to know more about the PPL (H) itself.

The PPL (H) can be likened to a driving licence. It is the basic qualification that all helicopter pilots achieve first, whether that is the goal in itself or whether they are moving onto a career in flying. The PPL (H) entitles you to fly as Pilot In Command (PIC) of a helicopter, with passengers, in daylight and in reasonable weather conditions. You can fly to other countries, and day trips to the continent are easy for someone based in the south-east of the UK. Flying magazines are filled with PPLs making trips to airfields in the far corners of Europe and beyond, although in fairness this is more rare for helicopters than for fixed-wing aircraft. Perhaps more importantly, helicopters do not need an airfield, and can land at hundreds of 'helipads' throughout the country, places not accessible to a fixed-wing aircraft. Many of these helipads are attached to hotels, restaurants and country clubs, and it is such 'point-to-point' flying that is the essence of travelling in helicopters. Helicopters can also, in principal, land at any suitable site based on private land, subject to the permission of the landowner.

The PPL (H) is valid in most countries of the world (sometimes with some paperwork formalities), so you can hire helicopters around the world, although insurance requirements are often more onerous than the country's certification procedures.

You do not have to buy your own helicopter once you have completed the PPL (H) course, indeed the majority of PPLs do not have their own helicopter. You should be able to hire a helicopter from the flying school you learnt

A Bell 206 Jet Ranger, a popular touring helicopter

with, who may also have more advanced touring helicopters that you can move up to, which are faster and have increased capacity. The only real limit is that of how much money you are prepared to spend. No-one pretends that flying helicopters is a cheap pastime, although it has become far more affordable, particularly in the last decade.

The PPL (H) itself is valid for life, and there is no need for you to take another test or exam once you have it. However, to use your PPL (H) there are two main requirements:

> Medical – you must have a current medical certificate (described shortly)
>
> Currency – you must fly at least 5 hours every 13 months, and have your logbook endorsed as proof.

Clearly these requirements are not onerous, and most pilots fly more than the legal minimum.

As already stated, most pilots do not own their own helicopter, but you should not think that is unavoidably expensive to do so. A used two-seater helicopter, such as the one you would learn on, can probably be purchased for around the cost of an up-market luxury car. Of course, there is virtually no upper limit to what you can spend on a helicopter, you should be able to pick-up a very desirable 5 seat type for no more than a million pounds or so.

There are several thousand airfields and helipads throughout Europe, so you will never be short of places to visit. There are also several hundred flying events each year in the UK alone, a number of which are specifically for helicopters. Flying events in general vary from the informal 'fly-in' at a small airstrip or helipad, where you can literally drop in for a chat, to much larger or more organised events such as major air displays where visitors by air are spared the traffic jams before and after the show. The use of a helicopter may also give you easy access to non-aviation events such as horse races, motor races etc., and it really is difficult to beat the 'one-upmanship' of arriving at such an event flying your own helicopter.

The annual Popular Flying Association rally

For many pilots, the PPL (H) itself is just a basic qualification onto which they add various additional ratings and qualifications. Two of the most popular are:

> The Night Rating – entitling the holder to fly by night.
>
> The Instrument Rating – an instrument flying qualification entitling the holder to fly in cloud and poor visibility, use radio navigation aids and make instrument approaches to land in a suitably equipped machine.

Many schools also offer instruction in mountain flying. Although this does not lead to a rating as such, it is a new challenge and a new set of skills to acquire.

In reality, the PPL (H) allows a pilot to take flying as far as he or she wants, to coin a cliché, the sky really is the limit!

Pre-Entry Requirements

There are no formal pre-entry requirements for starting the PPL (H) course. You should be basically literate and numerate, but there is nothing in the course or exams that will burden anybody without advanced educational qualifications. There is no minimum age for learning to fly, although any flying time gained prior to the age of 14 cannot be counted towards the course requirements. You cannot fly solo until you are 17, but at the other end of the scale there is no maximum age for learning to fly or holding a PPL (H). Before being able to fly solo you must have passed a medical with an Authorised Medical Examiner – the flying school will be able to give a list of local AMEs. The medical for a PPL (H) is nothing more complicated than an average life insurance medical, and is valid as below:

Aged under 40	5 years
40 – 49	2 years
50 – 69	1 year
70 and over	6 months

You can only fly as Pilot In Command (e.g. without an instructor or qualified pilot) if you hold a valid medical certificate. If you have any queries about the medical and its requirements it is a good idea to contact an AME, or the CAA's Medical Division, at an early stage.

The PPL (H) Course

As we saw at the beginning of the book, the flying time of an introductory lesson counts towards the flying hour requirements of the Private Pilot's Licence (Helicopters) course. The course itself consists of a minimum number of flying hours (currently 40), together with a certain amount of ground work to pass five short multi-choice examinations on subjects such as Air Law, Meteorology, Navigation etc.

You should realise at the outset that you do not have to sign up for a full course in order to start learning to fly. You can book lessons as often (or as rarely) as you like, and you can pay for each lesson as you take it. In the early stages each lesson will be of about an hour duration, although once the cross-country navigation stage of the course is reached longer flight times are necessary. There is no calendar time limit for completing the course. Somebody who can commit themselves full-time to the course can probably complete it in four weeks. For those who are flying in their spare time, anything from 9 to 18 months is closer to average. Ideally you should try to fly at least every 2 weeks or so (more frequently if you can), especially in the early stages. If your lessons are too far apart you may find that you have to spend time in the air just revising previous exercises before you can progress. Bear in mind too that the weather plays an important role, especially in the early stages of the course. Flying in poor weather is a waste of your time and money and no reputable school will encourage you to get airborne if the weather makes it likely that you cannot properly complete the lesson.

Simply starting flying lessons in no way obliges you to complete the course. Many people start with the aim of simply seeing how things progress, or trying to master the hover, or perhaps aiming for the first solo; and there is nothing wrong with that. Many flying schools offer various schemes of block-booking and pre-payment which reduce the cost of lessons and these are worth considering.

Aside from the flying itself, the school will probably have evening lectures for the examination subjects which are integrated with the flying syllabus. You will need certain training materials as you progress – a logbook, maps, text books, navigational equipment etc. The school can advise you what you need and when to buy it, and most flying schools carry a stock of this equipment. Many schools also have a reasonably active social side, and even when you are not flying you will find many pilots and trainees around.

The next flying lesson after the introductory lesson is Exercise 4 (the Effects of Controls), which explores in more detail not just the principal flying controls you will have used in the introductory lesson, but the ancillary controls too. You will then progress through more straight and level flying, climbing, descending, turning and hovering. This will lead you into the 'circuit', where you will practice take-offs and landings. Then comes the moment when your instructor steps out of the helicopter and sends you off for your first solo flight. This is truly a never-to-be-forgotten moment, even veteran pilots with a lifetime of flying behind them will be able to tell you when and where they made their first ever solo flight.

More circuit flying follows, practising different take-off and landing techniques and more advanced hovering manoeuvres, interspersed with more solo flying. This leads to map reading and navigation flying, which culminates in cross-country flights, in which you fly away from the home airfield to land at another point at least 25 nautical miles distant.

After some revision, you will take the Flight Test. This is a flight of around 1.5 hours with an examiner (often the school CFI), who you may well have flown with before. The Flight Test consists principally of flying the manoeuvres and demonstrating the techniques that you have learnt throughout the course.

With the Flight Test and ground examinations passed, the school will assemble a small pile of paperwork relating to your training course and exams, help you fill-out the relevant forms, and the whole lot (together with a cheque for the CAA) disappears towards a large glass atrium just outside Gatwick Airport, which is the headquarters of the CAA. In return you will get the coveted piece of paper, your PPL (H), that opens-up the world of helicopter flying to you.

Some of the text books available for the PPL course

Appendices

Abbreviations & Glossary

Apron	The part of the airfield where the helicopter is normally parked
ASI	Airspeed Indicator
ATC	Air Traffic Control
AVGAS	AViation GASoline – the fuel used by small helicopters
Book-out	The process of notifying ATC or the airfield operator of the proposed flight
CAA	The Civil Aviation Authority, responsible of regulating flying in the UK
Canopy	The clear 'bubble' area around the cockpit
Carb.	Carburettor
CFI	Chief Flying Instructor
Circuit	The traffic pattern around the airfield for helicopters arriving and departing
Coaming	The 'shelf' on top of the instrument panel
CPL	Commercial Pilot's Licence
Crosswind	A wind blowing at an angle across the runway or the flight path of the helicopter
Finals	The approach to land
HI	Heading Indicator
Holding Point	A point close to a runway where a helicopter stops before entering or crossing the runway.
Knot	One nautical mile, a speed of 10 knots is 10 nautical miles per hour.
Mph	Miles per hour
PIC	Pilot In Command – during the introductory lesson the instructor is the PIC
PPL (H)	Private Pilot's Licence (Helicopters)

PTT   Press To Transmit, the radio transmit button

QFE   (Quebec Foxtrot Echo) The pressure setting on the altimeter sub-scale which allows the altimeter to read <u>height</u> above the airfield

QNH   (Quebec November Hotel) The pressure setting on the altimeter sub-scale which allows the altimeter to read <u>altitude</u> above sea level

Tech. log   Technical log, forms and logbooks individual to a helicopter in which all it's flights are recorded

Threshold   The beginning of the runway, where the runway numbers may be painted.

The Phonetic Alphabet

The 'phonetic' alphabet, in which each letter is given a name and specific pronunciation, is used extensively in aviation, not just on the radio. The table below gives the phonetic word and pronunciation for each letter:

Letter	Phonetic Word	Pronunciation
A	Alpha	**AL** FAH
B	Bravo	**BRAH VOH**
C	Charlie	**CHAR** LEE
D	Delta	**DELL** TAH
E	Echo	**ECK** OH
F	Foxtrot	**FOKS** TROT
G	Golf	GOLF
H	Hotel	HOH **TELL**
I	India	**IN** DEE AH
J	Juliett	**JEW** LEE **ETT**
K	Kilo	**KEY** LOH
L	Lima	**LEE** MAH
M	Mike	MIKE
N	November	NO **VEM** BER
O	Oscar	**OSS** CAH
P	Papa	PAH **PAH**
Q	Quebec	KEH **BECK**
R	Romeo	**ROW** ME OH
S	Sierra	SEE **AIR** RAH
T	Tango	**TANG** GO
U	Uniform	**YOU** NEE FORM
V	Victor	**VIK** TAH
W	Whiskey	**WISS** KEY
X	X-ray	**ECKS** RAY
Y	Yankee	**YANG** KEE
Z	Zulu	**ZOO** LOO

Useful Addresses

AOPA
>The Aircraft Owners and Pilots Association
>50a Cambridge Street
>London SW1V 4BR
>Tel: 0171 834 5631

BHAB
>British Helicopter Advisory Board
>Building C2, West Entrance
>Fairoaks Airport
>Chobham
>Woking
>Surrey GU24 8HX
>Tel: 01276 856100

CAA
>The Civil Aviation Authority
>Aviation House
>South Area
>Gatwick Airport
>West Sussex RH6 0YR
>Tel (Switchboard): 01293 567171
>Tel (Flight Crew Licensing): 01293 573580/1
>Tel (Medical Division): 01293 573685

Flyer magazine
>Flyer Magazine
>Third Floor
>3 Kingsmead Square
>Bath BA1 2AB
>Tel: 01225 481440
>e-mail: ians@seager.demon.co.uk

HCGB
>Helicopter Club of Great Britain
>Ryelands House
>Aynho, Banbury
>Oxfordshire OX17 3AT
>Tel: 01869 810646

PFA

The Popular Flying Association
Terminal Building
Shoreham Airport
Shoreham By Sea
West Sussex BN43 5FF
Tel: 01273 461616

Pilot magazine

Pilot Magazine
The Clock House
28 Old Town
Clapham
London SW4 0LB
Tel: 0171 498 2506
e-mail: 100126.563@CompuServe.com

Aviation on the Internet:

The following are a few sites on the Internet and CompuServe. Most have links that will take you to further sites:

Internet

Aerial Approaches	http://www.hiway.co.uk/aviation/aerial.html
Airplan Flight Equipment	http://www.airplan.u-net.com/
Aviators Network	http://www.aviators.net
Avweb Magazine	http://www.avweb.com
Flight Safety Foundation	http://rhytech.com/~fsf/
Helispot	http://www.helispot.com/
Popular Flying Association	http://www.hiway.co.uk/aviation/pfahome.html
Popular Rotorcraft Assoc.	http://www.pra.org

CompuServe

CIS: AVIATION (located via the travel icon on the CIM page). Two particularly useful forums are:

AVSIG forum

AVSUP forum

Index